ISBN: Softcover   978-1-7960-4469-0
        Hardcover   978-1-7960-4470-6
        EBook   978-1-7960-4468-3

Print information available on the last page

Rev. date: 07/10/2019

To order additional copies of this book, contact:
Xlibris
1-888-795-4274
www.Xlibris.com
Orders@Xlibris.com

DEDICATION

This book is dedicated to my daughter Amy Catheryn Gonzales (1972-2013). Amy was born with Down syndrome. I was told to think about putting her in an institution, but that was not an option for me and I soon realized, it was not an option for Amy either.

As Amy grew up, she became one of the most beautiful, happy, smart, humorous, talented people anyone would ever hope to meet. She was a Special Olympian; winning many gold medals, she could read and write very well, graduated from high school with her peers, and went through one year of college where she studied computer science. She also worked for a grocery store as a courtesy clerk for 17 years. Amy spent her extra time bowling, swimming, and coloring and painting beautiful pictures.

Amy was able to retire from the grocery store and moved out to live on her own in an Assisted Living Facility for persons who are intellectually or developmentally disabled. There she had her own apartment, gained her independence, made many new friends, and where she found her final happiness.

Amy will be forever loved, forever missed, and will never be forgotten.

ACKNOWLEDGEMENT

I would like to acknowledge the parents of children that were born with an intellectual or developmental disability (I/DD) for their support and encouragement.

They taught me how to fight my fears, they went through the grieving process with me, they educated me on integration, and how to become an advocate and a champion for all persons who are intellectually or developmentally disabled, so they would be socially accepted, educated, work in the community, and have full, satisfying lives.

Most of all, I want to acknowledge the children and adults with I/DD that I have met throughout my journey with Amy. They showed me that they can carry on their lives in happiness and love unconditionally. They choose to participate in life to their fullest ability, showing their talent, breaking barriers, and supporting each other.

I would also like to thank the educators, advocacy organizations, and professionals who provided me and other parents with the education and training on how to reach our goals for full inclusion of all children and adults with I/DD.

Amy sat on the front porch staring across the street at the two neighbor boys who were jumping up and down excitedly as they watched their race cars go around and around, faster and faster, around the curves on the figure eight race car track that was set up on the driveway.

Amy's heart began to pound with excitement, and suddenly she found herself walking across the street to watch the boys. "What are you guys doing?" She asked. The boys, Matt and Michael, turned and stared curiously at Amy and for a minute there was silence. "Oh, um, we're racing our cars," stammered Matt.

"I like race cars," Amy said suddenly as she rubbed her hands together, something she often did when she was excited. "Oh," said Matt as he looked over at Michael with a confused look on his face. Then Matt said to Amy, "Well, we have to go now." The boys picked up their cars and broke apart the race car track. They walked away as they talked about the figure eight race car tournament to be held in Cooperstown in just a few weeks. As the boys parted to go their separate ways, Amy stood in the middle of the sidewalk alone and looked sad. Michael turned and waved goodbye to her.

She walked slowly back across the street and sat down on the front porch. Her mother called from the window, "Amy, it's time for supper, come in now and after supper you need to practice your reading."

Amy and her parents moved to Denver from a small town in Colorado. It was difficult for Amy to leave her friends and she felt very lonely, but she needed a better school program; one that only a larger city could offer for Amy's disability. Amy was born with Down syndrome.

Since Amy did not have any friends, she spent most of her time learning how to read and write. It was difficult, but she worked hard on it every day and never complained. When she was not studying, she also loved to color, draw and paint.

While sitting at her desk, she often drifted off, remembering how her Uncle Tom would let her play with his huge race car track that was set up in the basement recreation room. She would race the cars around the track for hours while her Uncle Tom told her stories of how he won his trophies when he was a young boy.

Tinkering with her Uncle Tom's race car track became Amy's favorite pass time and she became very good at it. Her Uncle Tom began to call her Amy Eight Track. Everyone in the family was surprised by her ability to work the controls, how she concentrated, and her eye-hand coordination, which the doctor said would not develop very well.

It was a Saturday morning when Amy woke up to the sound of children playing and laughing. She dressed in a hurry, went to the front door and peeked out. Amy looked around for her mother and did not see her, so she ran out of the door, ran down the stairs and ran across the street. She sat down on the grass and was watching the boys play for a long time before she was noticed. Michael turned around and asked, "What's your name?" "Amy," she said. "You're new here huh?" "I see you get off of the special school bus," he said to her.

As Amy was nodding her head to say yes, she asked, "Can I play?" "I like to race cars." "Ok, I guess, but racing cars are for boys, not girls." He answered back. Michael gave her the controls and said, "Let's see what you can do?" The boys began to laugh, as though they were making fun of her.

Slowly, Amy walked up, took the controls, and began to play. Jimmy, Matt's older brother was surprised how well Amy was controlling the cars and at how much she knew. They were having so much fun; they did not realize it was way past lunch time. Amy soon became one of the kids on the block and the boys would argue over whose racing partner she would be.

On Friday, the day before the tournament, the boys were preparing for the big race when Matt became very sick. Michael was worried all day. He knew he could not enter the competition without a partner. He sat for hours thinking, and hoping Matt would get better, but he didn't. Suddenly, he thought to himself, Amy, Amy, maybe she could be my partner! Michael ran across the street to Amy's house. His heart was pounding as he knocked on the door hoping Amy's mother would allow her to go.

Amy's mother opened the door and saw the worried look on Michael's face. "Michael, what's wrong?" She asked. Taking a deep breath, he explained that Matt was very sick and could not go to the tournament. He asked if Amy would be able to go to Cooperstown to be his partner. Amy peeked out from behind her mother, but she did not fully understand what was going on.

"Amy," said her mother, "Michael wants to know if you can help him win the big figure eight race he and Matt have been practicing for?" "He needs a partner because Matt is sick, and he can't go." "Do you want to go?" She asked. Amy just shrugged her shoulders and said, "Yes, I can help Michael." "That's great!" Shouted Michael. "My mom will take us, so we'll pick you up at 8:00 in the morning, ok?"

The next day, Michael's mother drove them to the area where the racetracks were set up. Amy and Michael got very excited. Jimmy, Matt's older brother came along to help since Matt was home sick. When it was time for Michael and Amy's turn for the competition, Jimmy explained to Amy what she was supposed to do. Jimmy said very slowly, "ok Amy, the lights will flash yellow, then they will flash green and that means go!" Amy listened to Jimmy, but she also remembered everything her Uncle Tom taught her.

There had never been a girl in the competition before and Michael wasn't sure how it would go, but they were ready, and Michael knew Amy would do her best. Michael and Amy took their places, controls in hand, watching very carefully for the green light. And so, it began; around and around in a figure eight, up and down, the cars went faster and faster! Michael and Amy's cars were falling behind as the race was coming to an end. All the children were shouting, clapping, and getting involved in Amy's excitement. Jimmy shouted, "second place, you took second place!" "Way to go Amy!"

On the way home, Amy held the trophy. Knowing that the boys were proud of her put a smile on her face. As the car went down the highway, the boys talked about next year's tournament and although they were very tired, they playfully argued. "Next year, Amy will be my partner!" Shouted Jimmy. "No, Amy is going to be my partner!" Argued Michael. They laughed and told stories all the way home.

Amy was now accepted as a friend and a team member. She was no longer thought of as the girl across the street that has a disability.

The End

Printed in the United States
By Bookmasters